summonings

summonings

raena shirali

www.blacklawrence.com

Executive Editor: Diane Goettel
Cover Design: Zoe Norvell
Book Design: Amy Freels
Cover Art: "daayan unfurled, 2021" by Meera Dugal

Published 2022 by Black Lawrence Press.
Printed in the United States.

Contents

Foreword   I

+

daayan looks to the earth   7

+

on projection   II
summoning : you didn't submerge your head in the river   14
lucky inhabitant   16
ghazal against [declining to name the subject]   18
garba, *or* womb + lamp, *or* as in every tradition there is a woman
     & her body & both are vessels   19
ojha : rituals   20
the mountains recall the village's myth   22
we don't belong   23
to curse or to pray   24
the universe will end & kali will still be here   25
at first, trying to reach those accused   27

+

summoning : retreat   31
daayan senses the ojha   34
daayan gets her name   35
daayan after a village feast   36
the tea leaves   37
daayan, feet facing forward   38

daayan & the mountains : i   40

daayan conjures up a forest   42

one red thread through the middle   43

the village goddess talks to herself while applying kohl   45

summoning : you are not a myth   46

daayan at gold streak river   48

+

before plantations, women rustle the brush together   53

the village men find some [fellowship], [hunt]   55

daayan imagines herself as the village goddess   56

the villagers' story   57

daayan & the mountains : ii   58

the mountains speak to the village   60

daayan summons the village goddess   61

summoning : chai & failure   62

summoning : wanderless   63

+

[every woman is a potential witch]   67

+

god of new beginnings, i celebrate you poorly   75

on persona   79

coldplay goes to india to shoot during holi & i just have to
     keep living my life   81

pastoral with keys clenched, as a weapon, in my fist   83

summoning : ways you asked for it   84

jodhpur, jharkhand, philadelphia   86

summoning : ash in my palms, ash on the streets   89

i make a toothpick diadem & crown myself token   94

summoning : second chakra   96

+

at home, in the empire   99

Notes   101

Glossary of Terms   109

Acknowledgments   110

Foreword

summonings investigates the ongoing practice of witch hunting in India—specifically, in Jharkhand & in migrant *adivasi* communities of tea plantations in West Bengal (though the phenomenon has also been documented in Madhya Pradesh, Chhattisgarh, & Bihar). As recently as October 2020, the very month in which I am writing this précis, articles noting the pervasiveness of witch hunting are being published by organizations like *Vice* & *BBC*. Individual states have passed protective legislation as recently as 2015, but these crimes, nonetheless, often go unreported & unpunished, due to mistrust of law enforcement & villagers' tendencies towards communal self-protection, among other factors. Some of the dynamics of the cultures of accusation that you encounter in this text will feel familiar; others may seem novel or difficult to fathom. But what ties them to you, reader, whoever & wherever you are, is the extent to which they are grounded in profound misogyny & the fact that these incidents are current & real.

These poems explore how antiquated & existing norms surrounding female mysticism in India & America inform each culture's treatment of women. More broadly, they ask: how do first- & second-generation immigrants reconcile the self with the lineages that shape it, in particular when those lineages are inextricable from misogynistic & violent narratives? My own parents immigrated from India to America four years before I was born; to that end—difficult as it is to navigate my two cultures' combating pressures—I am fascinated by parallels between their cultural norms. Expectations surrounding women's behavior coalesce in both countries' conceptions of marriage & the household. Netflix specials are made to highlight each nation's most horrific gang rape cases. As democracies, both nations purport to value equality, yet are sites of nationalist movements rooted in racist & colonialist ideologies—ideologies that, in both countries, have also involved literally hunting women as a means of maintaining patriarchal order. And in my own life, my unifying experience with both of my cultures is that in neither am I safe—that is, neither one is safe for women. Accordingly, my vision for this particular collection crystalized upon encountering *Thomson Reuters'* findings from June 25, 2018: [India is the world's most dangerous country for women due to the high risk of sexual violence...according to a poll of global experts...The only Western nation in the top 10 was the United States, which ranked third when respondents were asked where women were most at risk of sexual violence, harassment and being coerced into sex].

Indebted to the docupoetics tradition, this book interrogates the shifting role of witness & the political implications & shortcomings of writing Subaltern personae while acknowledging my Westernized positionality. Holding central that an ethical poetics must be grounded in the inevitable failure to embody the Other, this book grapples with a query that resonated throughout my research, articulated here by scholar Ayesha Matthan: [How do we make sense of the overall dismal condition of Indian women—measured in terms of the sex-ratio, life expectancy, literacy, income, subjection to violence, equality of opportunity, legal equality, and societal attitudes towards her—in a society that worships the all-powerful goddess in her many forms?]. I offer you here no answers, but attempts; my failed conjurings, faint summonings. The smell of ash in wind—I follow it.

Throughout this collection, brackets indicate language sampled directly from anthropological research.

Daayan(s): women accused of being witches; [selected women do not fit one profile], but all are [branded as the potential keepers of evil spirits].

Ojha(s): [medicine men, the ones next to God, religious ministers or priests who deal with the daily struggles of the village people]; this dynamic allows ojhas to control the circulation of rumors, & he is the village member who has the power to trap daayans.

"Any woman's death diminishes me."

Adrienne Rich, "From an Old House in America." 1974.

daayan looks to the earth

they say we're married to dirt, ground-bound & sure
to bend. break these bones & call us miracle, kiss our feet

then call us backward. sisters, when will we braid
our hair despite their songs? i gather seeds

from alluvial beds, save tamarind peels &
pepper stems & cardamom pods. who's to say

what will ward off or invoke? our name
wasn't given. doesn't have to mean *tie us to the deep & save*

the men. once, [dain], [dakani], [daayan]
sounded like fingers brushing reeds apart, meant wisdom

beyond keeping them fed. sisters, they starve us
& call us hungry bitches, kill us & call us

undead. come with me to these central rooms,
our lineage—flowering harvest & the machine we built

to feast through monsoons. smell that raindark,
that incense rimmed with milk? that's us.

deserving a true feast. let's toast. to our own next
good thing. to faith in shoots, our unsung roots.

+

"I keep praying and asking my goddess 'what is my crime?'"

Accused woman, Bahura Bai. 2013.

on projection

the gun to my head is ownership.
the gun to my head is
i'm taking the word *empathy*
& hanging it as on a laundry line
& watching it waver in wind
& not believing in words & also
relying on them. reader, men & women alike
shutter themselves with superstition.

+

supposing i board
the plane, remain suspended

some sort of cloud,
buoyant, detached

for one full day, followed by my arrival
in a place not

of my mother's dialect, not
of my father's kin, armed

with language : [patrilineal],
[marang buru], [flower feast], [nage era].

how surely i'd arrive with detriments : visible
tattoos, hair dyed lighter at the ends, english

a target pinned to the chest, the west,
        the inescapable truth of my birth.

+

to explain the distance
between self & subject is to admit
the unlikelihood of my self
understanding a given subject. i'm talking : theorizing

understanding. i'm talking :
my inevitable failure to embody.
reader, consider
the basic elements of this narrative—daayan, ojha : hunted,

godly. assume
telling any story fully
involves considering all sides.

+

here, men wield village secrets
like weapons, catapult accusations
through the fields. i've read so much

about legs & backs : ache-laden
& no choice but to eat [paje] daily
& yet—.

i'm just camera. i'm shutter, closed, i'm protected
from light, i'm just telling a story
to which i'll never know an end.

+

no boarding the plane

no bitter root

no lean season

no poem

summoning : you didn't submerge your head in
the river

first, thread your lashes with lace & shells, paint
your nipples with drying mud, watch the cells flake
off your gold-wracked body

+

it's true you used to look at skin
darker than yours & see your posture straighten

it's true you're ashamed of your bird cage, your glass
year, your short shorts & tan lines

+

what if you were a gold bangle placed on a holier woman's
nape? ring around the cord around the
touch me my skin is a glisten you'll call :

+

what if you were the paint smeared
across your own   cheeks?

+

so you say to the birch skeleton in the bathroom mirror
unravel me i'm all this stuff of the earth. the mirror could be
laughing, saying   *girl, in my light*
you're just another imagined   another unmarried

+

you say *touch me i'm the bronzer*
like there isn't all this death in here

+

welcome to the country of white sheets
& white bird cages, of everything-tasseled-is : of everything-
holy : the already-dead, your absence

lucky inhabitant

failing to conjure even distant relatives   i know not

which women precede me, believe all this pain is at least
our own   on my lap   experts theorize

[witchcraft is no longer a personal matter]

state plainly [the women had nails
driven into their foreheads] & full up now with steel

& scythes & a list of weapons wielded

against us, am nauseous & taking it   personally   though
at least am not asked to detail my assault on television

holding my chin up for photographers   dubbed *icon*

& simultaneously driven out of the nation
yes   you might say this makes me one of the lucky

inhabitants   yes   here there are no [jackfruit

trees] but in a chamber the semicircle of [men had red
eyes—the kind of eyes that saw no reason and were filled

with cruelty] & somewhere online i am blamed

for not remembering   yes   gone now my willful ascension
the stairs, his room   & i don't fight back   know what fate

        awaits women who protest too much   no matter dialect

or country the question is the same   [*ki jani*]   they ask
in the motherland   & *who knows*   here we throw up

        our hands & it isn't in prayer

there's blood in the soil so they call it *filth*   blood
on our legs so they call us *gone*   they're not wrong

        & they will not   be fooled, won't   take it back

it's night & the [jackfruit trees] close in   there's chanting
in the distance who owns   this world

ghazal against [declining to name the subject]

Bahura Bai, it matters that you have a name. that you live
past the story : you were young,

Teerath Sahu, chased out of your home by twelve or more friends,
men, family, called [antisocial], [killer]. younger

still, the children falling sick, cattle keeled over, growing
rancid in yearlong heat, buried as afterthought. in your own youth

you thought daayans real. [the process of attraction—the power of girls
to inflame passion, to subdue boys at their will] made your young skin

prickle. here, there is no archetype ungendered. & blood like yours,
like mine, doesn't stay profitable long. & i'm too young

to be telling your story, & privileged, & the rain keeps falling
like the sky's own mountain, your youths

hiding under their cot, your husband accused of sheltering you—.
Jaam Bai, there is only more terror. gone, now, those youthful

days the men would stop by your house, ask for rice, for roots.
even then, the killing had begun. no one here, at last, stays young.

garba, *or* womb + lamp, *or* as in every tradition there is a woman & her body & both are vessels

toenail polish warped waxen from sand, you leave
your body behind again : mere rind, edges buzzing
from unsought touch. you end up in a skeleton

house & on a driveway with the sun
holding vigil : that central flame, her silent
drumming. her reminder : you could, if you flared, contain

something alive. instead you skin your bare soles
raw shuddering up & up the drive. you are so many girls
trying to move unbridled, you forget yourself. you wretch & tear,

o only repentance   o patriarchied psyche : split
in perpetuity : once you stood barefoot
on linoleum eating something delicious

out of the jar. it was the year of your favorite
animal, the year of mosquito nets canopying
your twin sized heart. you jostled your ankles

to hear a tinkling, you sent your arm
heaving to twist your body in a circle
of women that never breaks. those women

never broke formation. those women
who made you, who taught you the footwork,
its weave & lilt, but never   how to run.

ojha : rituals

certain beliefs precede his name & yet
he goes by many. [dewar], [bhagat],

priest. passive ear, the kind

of listener you'd give
your own face.

+

first, the village must [agree
that spirits exist]. some benevolent,
some deserving of fear. everyone

wants their universe
to have reason. so it must be
a woman who stole your portion

of rice, woman who smeared
your doorstep's rangoli, woman
who looked sideways at your child.

+

give him your gossip & the ojha conjures
herbs to [appease] [evil] : her raving,
innocent mouth. & by that token
what is truth. other rumors,

too, corroborate : that bullets
pass through, his body barely
there but for the holy
in his hands.

+

he chants her name with fingers
pushed into his ears. just the [sound
of her bangles]
undoes : a single woman

on a plot of land, unbecoming.
he reads her guilt [in grains
of rice, in the light of a lamp,
using a cup which moves

and identifies]. makes a circle
around himself. white sand
between him &
the world. it's the dead hour.

now, he shouts, arms covered
in ants, *sing.*

the mountains recall the village's myth

i remember you insisted : the [sacred grove] virile : no place
                    for a girl's bare feet. you hoarded language
        because you knew words spin

in pliant hands : bound : divined : grains of rice
                    scattered : lantern shadow shaped
        like a woman. & tell me who had power

first. who turned walking home
                    into a setup. so you didn't expect blood
        on their calloused palms. all everyone's trying to do

is survive. the trees hide such small chirpings, such invisible
                    animals : women catch or pluck what they can
        because they know that berry & seed are no

guarantee. granted, dupattas tucked behind ears, who knew
                    what fire they stoked & why. mortals, you said
        they tricked the wisdom from you, said when the river

rose they drowned, but i saw their bodies in the reeds, saw
                    your bodies glistening with what you called
        holy. bhaiyas, remember, none of us asks to be born.

we don't belong

in rooms with family spirits : central on blueprints

near rivers where one could be caught : submerged

with our teeth sunk in thighs : with our thighs visible to a flash of teeth

licking milk off our mouths' edges

near gold : paint : pearls or oysters

straight-backed & sure : close to the horizon : some drop-off point

in classrooms : learning about the end of the world

contemplating heat : dipping ring fingers in turmeric & slaked lime

asking about symbols : patterns in sand

asking *but do we worship the violent goddesses?*

calling each other *queen* like it undoes the fact of their stares

next to our husbands : together in rivers : baring our teeth at the stupid sun

calling it blood lust : killing us across oceans

blessing kali's foot on her man's neck : tongue thrust out

    even our idols were made to feel shamed

to curse or to pray

bless us with fertility for she has chosen ash : o how
many sickles must we survive : she bares her shining
teeth & there isn't any moonlight : we don't see her
drink the demon's blood : there's fury & then
wickedness dancing on her tongue : we only see her
taste her lover & want more : her tools all split &
strangle : dagger, drum, noose : she is the first of her
kind to show us her weapons : this is why we call her
dark one : bless the creative drive : endless new ways
to kill : her shield bears the likeness of a row of
pulled teeth : strung between cowry shells : jagged
necks, frayed ends : because she is violent we call her
lust : we mean what must it feel like : to taste your kill :
to move : possessed : by one's own black tongue : o
how much wanting must we witness in the tea fields :
we say *head on a stick* & look at her, pretending not to
listen : she trident : she cup of spilled soil : take her
song as proof : she's swaying in the reeds : [*i have cut the
plantation grove / i have taken off my clothes / i have learnt
from my mother-in-law*] how to sharpen one's teeth

the universe will end & kali will still be here

solo, skirting the rim of our smolder, our ruin,

all lotus bud, bell-beat & drum-song, those many hands &
the severed heads they hold, masc-demonic,

a warning. alone in the neither

light nor dark, she will stay the dusty blue
of not-time, will evade even as she creates,

is death & is energy, is. i cannot imagine

this : outliving one's infamy. how women
survive being burned alive & offer, in return,

forgiveness. girls with reconstructed faces

refusing hate. i want to crown all victims
the safety of fur, give each

our own grove, something sacred, i want

to worship dichotomy. o goddess of lust
& violence, i tire of trying to find peace.

i want to unleash. to unearth

rage. kali, we lived & our bodies were
trespassed. release us from this cage.

at first, trying to reach those accused

i swallowed burnt matchsticks, her hair a tar tumbleweed
in the room's south-facing corner. i did this to pray & i did this
to feel. & then i swallowed my old chant : his name, his
name : like i'm not made of my oppressor's
undoing. & then i swallowed theory. i swallowed
plantation politics, tried prying plantains from my lips, plump
from sitting on a velvet couch & touching them dry
to my wrists while reading about her body. strung up
for slaughter, called names in the oppressor's
language, covered in silt. & then i swallowed puddles. & then i
swallowed sandalwood & tried to cloak & cover
& render her erotic, for the oppressor sometimes saves
the objects of his desire.
           & then i swallowed desire. i held the smoldering
cow dung patty at my core. i smelled like it. i was shit & wanted
to be shit. & then i swallowed pretense. swallowed
countries. why try to get close when you could become, i said,
& then i swallowed myself, chased me down
with goat milk & shorn fur. & then i turned to the page
& swallowed it & i took it like a shot & took it like a man & took
the punches & still wandered through mazes of huts asking my people
what it felt like to be oppressed. & then i swallowed tea. i swallowed
the fertilized soil. & then i swallowed braids

& locust shells & i wanted to smell like incense
because the oppressor values patchouli & cedar
so i bought a candle to smell like my heritage
& then i swallowed wax & was viscous & suddenly then
i could not move. & my ankles were bound but they left my wrists
free. & i could not speak but still
i mouthed a name i'd never heard & i felt her
like my own ghost. there was no magic : it was not profound.

"They want to kill me. They believe I'm a sorcerer. In prayers, I ask my goddess every morning, 'am I really?'"

Accused woman, Bahura Bai. 2013.

summoning : retreat

digging in
the old-world soil
for common root,
i admit i'm
biological
disconnect, one
sole lime, unripe
in the green. if
you were here,
sister, you'd take
sugar in tea, sip
& dab, shiver
in the artificial
indoor. let me
introduce you to
some parts
of this place.
just there, men
hold guns like
newborns. &
there, a killer
caught by blood
he left on screens.

& here is where
i stand
on a porch
in the verdant
country &
say, *fuck the trees*
either stuck or
reaching for
nothing, lies
our poems
have told us of
greenery &
wishing. to no
one i write, *my life*
is spitting me
out of it. i am
the absence of
sound under
floorboards in
this house.
if they want us
to be visible
we will be
invisible.
if they want
to consume us

we will become
sharper knives.
sister, i'm through
with the world's
unblinking eye.
you don't have to
tell me earth
is all we have
to connect to.
even in such
a privileged space
i've seen
what men can do.

daayan senses the ojha

i don't want to call it *emergency*
      when i wake in a blue fog, the kind with orange
            edges : night's failed go at totality. except the orange

isn't morning. & night isn't total
      because of the flickering. & if i stretch out my arm
            all i'll hit is the left side of the cot. he's only been dead

a few weeks but already they call me *unthinkable*
      hunger. & since when are sadness & sin
            the same? before i met him in the tea fields, before

we married, i was just like them. i fell asleep
      with all my fingers crossed, looped together against
            the omen they name me now. i believed something

about safety & do-gooding & a universe that writes
      itself, favors the center. i was a cheerful fool. each day
            their torches near the threshold & i stay sated. i don't

want to call it *emergency,* but i know what will happen
      when they cross. i know what to call that color
            at the ashen edges of night.

daayan gets her name

& so what if they think they've found language befitting
my inexplicable, can't-be-pinned, my hair so black it defies

synonym? tongues move to the roofs of mouths to push
against teeth every day without realizing

what's been said. or maybe i'm too focused on the name,
the way they're too focused on the length

of my toes, fingernails, whether that's dirt or blood
crusted underneath. maybe the epithet is a fancy kurti

adorned with small circular mirrors that i get
to put on, like how it was being a wife

or a mother. just a different way to look at the same
old face. men have never understood that

about us : they'll think by *us* i mean daayans
but you know i mean *us* : women : mistaken

for all kinds of foliage. grasping root. wilting petal. gentle
weed. maybe i mean to say i am tired of being called

anything. i mean to say i am no plant, no witch,
but the hard surface of a cold rock. i'm fine falling

into some old cliché about my blood, when it decides
to follow oceans. that's why i'm here, asking this river

to let me float   away.

daayan after a village feast

any way to the bottom of a bottle is one the men
    will pioneer. moonlit paths through the pale green
        growth. they trade tea leaves, tobacco, ghee. they trade

what we women toiled. naturally, we sneak sips, dilute
    the remainder like kids, slinking on packed mud, careful
        not to step too heavy. i'm the only one who takes

full flasks like this. that's not why they want
    my pasture. they don't know their own skin
        glows amber : we all sweat it out the same.

teeth slump against gums. bones
    whittle down. maybe they feel bright yellow
        in their lungs, the unsung chakra, & think it's my fault

their feet slur the dirt. they pull me in with spindly
    arms, kiss me flat on the forehead, [haria]
        breathing their half-lie : how capable they are

of love. moments before the blackout, all their limbs
    ablaze, the whole world must seem possible & warm
        & fused. it must be intoxicating

to survive. they pass out unarmed, sloughed against fences,
    so we slip bottles from loose fists, tuck them into our
        baskets. we become mist, shift groveward, flee.

the tea leaves

i like to be handled mostly by anyone
but they say women's hands are nimbler, pluck me fast
from my hold. so it's women i'm with
when i'm bathed in yellow or blue or gray. how

could i believe in a world less visible : the air
coconut oil & sweat : their hair tied
& glistening through afternoon? what's real
if not their rough hands on my neck? one sings

under her breath, tracing a bend through stalks.
unadorned, they toss me in a basket with the rest
of myself. it's nothing like violence, like being driven
out of one's home. no, here i'm remade

essential, weightless. what's real if not
their basket-indented waists, what's real
if not their knees, how someone else decides
when to force them to the earth?

daayan, feet facing forward

peppers & lemon rinds sway in doorways
though i was bred just over their thresholds
& my hair isn't kept in a braid. kids hunch

behind bins, stare as i walk by. i know
what they're thinking. witch, man-eater, lonely
hag. my husband in ashes, my home next

to burn. all this doubling. it's no wonder
the villagers think of signs, lust after my land
as though it's anybody's to take. as though

when they slit the last girl's throat in the woods,
i simply sat by, not feeling a thing, not flinching
awake every night thereafter. let me dispel each

rumor, make each ember fade to floating
ash : look : i move with something akin
to grace : no backward-facing feet : no taste

for flesh. what would i want with these men
anyway? there's too much else out here
to love : the air smells bright : shells of pepper

twirl with abandon. they can't tell me i'm not
beautiful, smiling up at the deep maroon skins,
the ones meant to ward me off. already they're

saying, *she's killed her own kind.* bhaiyas, am i not
your own making, your own undoing? the breeze
warms. my sky smells alive. talk is talk. i will not die.

daayan & the mountains : i

but would you call it thirst?

> when i look closely, the cowry shell is just as jagged
> as my own pulsing, my own hunger

as in, you tongue salt off their edges?

> or roll them for luck. even then, there's no faith
> in that bet

would you call that thirst?

> you ask me like i know its opposite

& what if you are the myth?

> what if i were just a water-laden
> fragment? what then?

did a child die?

> the shoots weren't tender. i could only
> watch as they grew too tall

will the women come for you?

> they treat it like fact instead of rumored blood

but i'm not a prophecy
or prediction

would you call that thirst?

sometimes i lip dew from the edges. after all,
this is my land

daayan conjures up a forest

it is night again. the woods are verdant, marshy,
wet. somehow, crops dry anyway. this story
is depressingly old. where mud sinks into river, i sit
with a bottle i'm not allowed to buy. i can't remember
where it came from. i can't remember why i'm sitting
in the woods with a drink. but since i'm here
i'll make the trees, the bushes, give green
a rest. try red instead. try fire the women
in my family called *mark of a changed girl*. try palash,
gift from yet another goddess, & our lady
of power at that, *she from the mountains, born again*
after a man shamed her & she couldn't bear
to live any longer. i wish i didn't know
this story : the baddest woman burning
for some man. forget rebirth. forget parvati, sati,
any mysticism making us smolder. give me flowers
budding gray, whole fields of softly shaking grasses,
daylight devoid of hue. let there be no sign of blush, love,
anger : i want absence, less-ness,
static : a landscape colored so dismally, even i
can't shock it awake.

one red thread through the middle

levels of remove dart & are topography   & yes we
both can't choose   how to pray in a place like these

dry wells & governments fully in the know

passing laws for the cows & laws for their gods
no space in between for a woman   no space in between

for the fact   is a statistic   a graph   something reduced

to the trivial   how we all live next door
to someone & in the morning they may or may not

be in the mood for greeting   it's as if the language

need not be shared   but here i am not sharing
your tongue   if there were such a thing as a universal

gesture   to facilitate understanding is to make oneself

vulnerable   you're there standing in a field
in your grandmother's salwar   it's loose & smells faintly

of urine   of fabric softener   of vicks vapo rub

i know this   i have my own   it's the same   distant
chime   someone has won a game show   someone else

has died & the death not called *murder*   i declare i'm here

      to investigate   but this field is one of ash   the days
      have all burned down   & silly me   i keep being told

it's not safe to be here   go home

the village goddess talks to herself while applying kohl

: it's not my fault : it happened in the reeds : their awakening : me stringing

cowry shells with a dull needle : sweat-glorious & the gnats' quiet

hum : sometimes men want to see red : sometimes they see a pale

ankle & think : *wilt* : that day who knows why

they gathered : a loose crescent approaching : scythe without

a spine : other women will talk : but i felt my throat

unshut : heard : my own voice : ooze with gold : & before

i knew it : i was singing : not moving my body : no loose

spark at dusk : just offering a simple prayer : i thought :

maybe holy is all they need : someone : to believe in : just

coincidence i : wore my best face that day : just coincidence they

think nothing's : sublunary : every day now : i'll put on

this other mask : won't ask : why they think me

blinding : bright : some omen : in the dirt :

summoning : you are not a myth

& regardless you were raised on stories of good women
so you know the third time's the nip at your
heels the swing in your step the charmed life
you've been saying you don't want

+

you sit around all day with your desire, chant

auspicious, auspicious
that the sun won't come

+

moonlight sizzles dew off your neck. a man
squats by the bank, scoops mud into a little pile
at his feet. he packs it into a kind of snowball

& you can't look away. he licks silt
off his fingers. when it's too late, he tells you
to duck

+

hold your own ears shut
by folding the lobes up with your pointer fingers

that's it

hold them

+

if they fling stones & call you
a cold bitch, show them your nails
filed down

+

if they fling dirt & tell you
your body belongs here

rise

daayan at gold streak river

if at dusk the river's peach trembles into soot : if hip-thick
in mist i trace petals on waves : if the ripple slurs on : past

its outer limit : if the fact of my finger makes the sky
gild : if from a distance i look like a ghost : it's because i'm out here

with my ghosts : if the men yell [*bongas*] : suspect our flush
places wax carnal : if plumes off the shoreline mean *that's our earth*

killing again : & we know about killing : about twine
binding ankles to a thin branch : if my ghosts tell me how

they lived : morning sizzling dew off the shrubs :
the smallness of a tea leaf in a hand : the power to crush or fray

a living thing : fiber by fiber : if i say to one *it's getting*
dark : & she turns her head toward me : backlit

by gold streak : says, *but you are the matron of water* : her eyes
pepper-swollen : limbs thick with sinking : if the castor plant

grazed her skin nightly : if we float : if we float : if we float
& soak the lentils & follow the field's rows & if we came here

as brides & they threw us a feast : said *welcome* : *sisters,*
i say, *here we are at the end of the earth* : if the sky immolates: magenta

rimming the day as it dies : if it looks hopeless : if it is
hopeless : on the shore men jeer

    & hurl branches : if we don't turn back : if we wade out
together : cursed women : & find mountains instead

"We still shiver when we see those men roaming the village."

Accused woman, Teerath Sahu. 2015.

before plantations, women rustle the brush together

cloth slings bursting with nuts & berries, wound
around a length of bamboo. here, daayans forage, are
but women. they sit together,

feet dangling over roadside ditches, sharing stories of men
who stand almost too tall, craning their necks skyward
as if to project a peacock's air : male bird : all preen

& chosen. there are warnings. of villagers
who make shadows broad
as buildings. what did it mean to sit alone

or in groups? a woman lights a candle
& my imagination is a failure.
or a woman sits alone, cheeks red with sweat

& the color *red* doesn't signal. there
are solitudes i don't have
to interpret : no metaphor

for her joy. & if i am
aligned with anyone,   anyone
in jharkhand, how can i say it's not

with men : shaded safely at a distance
making observations : here : the art of taking
note.

the village men find some [fellowship], [hunt]

system says we're not in charge of much else
but this. system's [planter's raj] & the damn
tea. [the brits] sell us, [lipton] sells us, [tata]
sells us. when are we permitted to unload?

system says when crops dry, some liquid
must let. there's the trance of their girlhood

songs. children hungry as ever in streets. &
as far as the eye can muster, those two-toned
leaves. system doesn't care to convince us
daayans exist. we see their [jaher era] : the only

plants here in bloom. system says the earth is
parched, & look who [fetches] our [firewood],

our [fruits, vegetables]. we know [the needs of]
our [community], gather to drink, discuss
the magic we see. when we go, the women
dress in our clothes, practice incantations.

what can we do but band together, find
some [fellowship], [hunt]? goats zag down

now-rocky slopes, using branches as footholds,
slipping anyway. no [high rainfall], no [red]
[soil]. this is the life we have all fallen into.
system says it's an [honor] to [serve].

daayan imagines herself as the village goddess

& even if i call myself
devi, they'll say i have a dark

side, a form not
linen-bound, one

that's slur & sway
& endless skin. it won't

matter : that the skulls
clinking together, grazing

my nipples, belonged
to killers. & will

they worry : my arrows
in the dirt, my skirt

made of thieves'
hands. i already

know this ruse
won't last. my

body : nothing
to them but ash.

the villagers' story

it happened while he was sleeping. always
does. daayan stripped slowly, watching herself
in a puddle. wavering & blurry. something
shimmered. or a solid form approached, parting

      the flamelight with still more
      unknowable. we heard the bonga start

to touch her. or her body looked
like it was being touched. it happened
because she caved to thirst. it happened because
she was naked in moondark. after, daayan

      was aglow, every invisible hair on her body leaning
      in the same direction. she squatted down

& shrieked. her hips led her into his room. then
daayan's tongue running the length of her husband's
middle bones, pausing above his heart
to record its beat. we heard her braid wrapped

      around her hips. toes where her heels
      should be. she bore through his ribs with just

her teeth, him asleep all the while. she chewed free
his heart, took it still dripping in her hands,
smothered it with chili & ghee & we all know

      what happened next.

daayan & the mountains : ii

when they called me drowner, said i crafted my own
illness, the air was thick enough
to choke on. my lungs their own waterlogged
boats, their own sinkings

how floods make of us a question mark

parvat, you're too high up to tell me you, too, don't fear
the water, the river

you want to ask if i would call it conjuring,
cresting up from night blue, that deep lonesome.
you want to know how to survive

listen : i burned the incense. i prayed
when i was told. no kali, no dakini, no woman
smiling through bloody teeth

mortals have always had their sacred
groves. their unknowable fears

but then why drink their rumors
into whirlpool? they forget how they sang me
the marriage song. even the women

betee, i rose the same way you've fallen :

suddenly the earth began to shift &

without warning, we turn on ourselves.

the mountains speak to the village

from here, you're just flecks
in the emerald. which i'd never say
to hurt you. i'm saying a hundred bodies
running through a field chasing one
wind-whipped mustard sari—.

what spectacle do you call
yourselves, swarm of termites
flooding a mossy beam? i'm not trying

to be picturesque. i'm trying to say
i was dead to this earth when i got here
but you? tanned arms swaying, you pluck
a weed from soil, grind it
between teeth like a pestle. mortal

you do not think yourself, mortal waving a branch
you've fashioned into a spear, if she sat with you
on the stone by the river & you felt something

inside you like a vine creeping
across your veins—. mortal, i'm telling you
all she did   was exist.

daayan summons the village goddess

at the altar, men must hover around you
strangely, squatting in the wet dirt, waiting
for a sign. they must praise your forehead,
sindoor traced from part to temple

just so, kumkum a perfect circle, so centered,
surely your aura must be pure. o, the jewel
you have called yourself, woman with light eyes,
woman i tended with, contended with,

how we laughed when the men couldn't keep
their gaze off you. now, they imagine you
too radiant. they're seeing pastel pink
emanate off you in waves. never

mind. i'm outside, in the rain, trailing fingers
through the mud to make sure you know
i was here. the puddles keeping me company
are dim mirrors. or maybe i'm the one

who's faded. inside, dark magic thrives on your fair
suns. they chant for you, bless the parts
of you inclined to destroy (old friend, can't
you see : all women crave a burning). brief silence

from beyond the trees. they shout
my name. i press a seedling
                        to the earth.

summoning : chai & failure

in the living room again, i cannot conjure
even the space i inhabit. rain for several

years & an exposé about flat-beaked birds
brushing themselves on sharpest rocks. wrought

of my own inertia, i cannot make the journey
across an ocean, spend my only remaining

cash on the tangible. i am foreign & so
nothing has ever made sense. i'm domestic

& so expected to understand. i let chai steep
for hours on the counter, forget the milk

& don't own sugar, & the cup tastes of bitter
rain & sheared rock. the cup is cold. the room

is empty. i create another version of myself
& congratulate for her persistence.

summoning : wanderless

so you aren't struck by lightning
& regardless this culture has no myths
about lit women anyway

+

the animal spooled in his own unwinding
calls you *mother* in some dreams

other times someone reads your palm
shaking their head, saying, *no stars*

align, no stars align

+

the sun decides you aren't worth it. it's true
the sky's chakra is never wrong : peach puddles
line the horizon. you dip your toes

in runoff, think of white divinations
soaring over a synth

+

broken, you won't eat the mango, say
you shouldn't eat what will stain

+

you sit at the mouth of the river
alone, like always, like you never have
before. it sounds like it's singing *please*

go   *please*   but you know
no one tells the dead they're not wanted anymore

"In the evening, they finally left us to die outside a Goddess Durga temple."

Accused woman, Teerath Sahu. 2015.

[every woman is a potential witch]

dear S----,

several countries away i stand in a strewn field : empty
                           milk cartons : sheared plastic : the wind
        having its way with it all. i'm thinking about

your ankles, the burns from rope & flame, how the wind might
                       or might not sway your body
     [hung up] from a [tree]. i think of blood rushing to the head

& remember : [sinking is the only proof of] your [innocence].
                   when they cut you down & your [bones]
     don't flinch, do they offer you a drink? left with my [arms]

[tied] to a headboard once, i asked the [man] in the next room
                 to bring me back some water. he returned
     with more   rope.   the joy   was in his return.

+

dear N---------,

      speaking   of patrol. do you   pin up tarp,
   spare cloth as curtains?   do lamps   like searchlights
      bounce   through the forest? you've heard
of women   [tied and put in a bag and thrown]

     to the riverbed, to breath :   its failure to struggle
  perpetually.   & yet.   your friends call some women
     goddesses : those who keep   conceiving   despite
the bodies.   are you   as i would be   addict-sick

     with revenge? here,   it is no longer   fashionable
  to be   fertile.   i would prefer   to be driven
    by blood lust.   i'd want   that justice.
          there is no   justice   in birth.

                +

dear _____,

over dinner & after several glasses of boxed wine i start
ranting about reproductive rights & your name
comes up because you may not know
the term but furthermore it's as though your land
is your child & it can so easily be torn
from you. i haven't raised a thing like you've tended
to your crop. girls here wear chokers & carry crystals
in their pockets. perhaps it's a sign we all feel safe
in the woods. what would you think of the western trend
toward prophecy. were you raised to believe
in ghosts. were you raised to think what's happening to you
is what you deserve.

+

dear R---,

      last night, dreaming i was a woman accused :

i never know when to shut my mouth. telling the villagers yes,
i ate my husband's heart like some grotesque myth
& touched myself under the moon in front of a puddle
to see how far from myself i could blur. thinking all pain must be
like getting a tattoo, numbing in its relentlessness, not considering
constant alteration. not considering pressure on the lungs
when drowned.

+

dear _____,

i wonder if you wish death
on the village ojha, if to do so would be

wrong. i might as well ask
how to assuage a season. no rice, no gruel, no

crops. even here, the damn
relentless sun. i'm here trying to picture

you, i want to say, *take our hands, bhaiya,*
as proof, i wish for you some

small belief, a tea light, maybe, a chakra
of chalk—.

              i can only think to invoke
gods. even or especially as i wish against it,

an ojha towers above you, cast
in too-bright shadow.

                            +

dear____,

i dream i'm there :

& you're teaching me to draw rangoli in chalk. we
make rounds, leaving budding lotus & pale yellow
light on each village threshold. we talk about
believing in spirits & ghosts but agree the word
[witch]   was invented   to capture.

or i lied, & we can't speak because language, but still
we end the day's ritual by sharing a tree stump
as a stool, packing dung & mud into round plates
or firm bricks. it's warm, & this is your land,
& no one   wants to take it   from you.

but do you dream :

& if so is it of your lost sisters. the smell of warm
ghee on naan. your mother's sandalwood soap. of
your husband who you did   not kill. you   did
not   kill.   you   did not   kill.

✝

"Here a woman has only to listen and not to act on her own."

Accused woman, Jaam Bai. Quoted in 2015.

god of new beginnings, i celebrate you poorly

no vendors or busted starfruit in my dreams
& i can't tell my own shell from a tamarind's. i know

not everyone is so
lucky. not everyone's tricked into unwinding

weeks of fast & fast & give. it's true i'm surviving
in the land of failed festivals, setting aside

whole days to pray. i have offered what i can
& know : it's not enough.

+

night did not fall with my heart in summer & i turned
toward smoke to feel less, spent my days discussing. *is it possible*

for a white partner to fully

see me. color : that spectrum : his eyes closed & groping
for what in the dark.

+

no violence in solitude : another mantra, a lie. i pace
the house followed by a cloud of mosquitoes.
i keep trying to reach you, sister. some would call that

endless searching *love*. you're in the dark
or you are your own source of light & either way
it is dusk or not when you leave

home, lamplight, shadow or glow
of yourself. if to be loved is to be seen,
to you i am holding out

                              my hand.

+

i repeat : we glow darkly.
my love turns from me, won't
say why.

+

nights, i am closest to you, sister. in
sobriety, making lists of our similarities,
a framed recipe of all

the clichés : the edges of everything
suddenly sharpen, guitar strings seeming
long thin knives, leaves harassed by wind

while they're just trying to vine themselves
to something stable. it's september & i wish
of this mind an eraser, september

& feet carry the body unwilling
to the pharmacy counter, september when i ask
to stop forgetting even as i pray

                              to black out.

+

other nights burrow
into sheets so white they're transparent,
the quilting underneath visible. this : a poor metaphor

for reading up on your village. you're there
being seen but only barely & for naught : i'm tracing
stitching with a nail, waiting to feel cut.

+

night & i walk down the street in the shadow
of him, protected. yes : security is an illusion.

yes : i feel secure, arrive home sometimes
unscathed. & of that, am ashamed.

+

no women are allowed to be
suns. no unfurling gold

behind a raindark cloud. no daayan
a metaphor, no goddess

for the sick. no woman in no country
is not fielding some nonsense

she didn't ask for. & without
my summoning, nonetheless, here

it is, invoked : the question
of asking. who gets to. who answers.

who is free—& where
—to speak.

on persona

        fledgling each time i attempt another

body, call it : *tired of my own
trauma,* the writing

        into   & the writing out of.   i want to sing

a song of escape, won't admit poetry's
formula : begin

        with an image, spiral out—.

           my many masks hang
from window latches.

        misnomer to call them

adornments. of these works as a whole,
i say, find here no monetary

        value. no cultural

clout. the papers declare the line-
break   dead   as i write into

        death : here is a scythe

& here a tree & here, me
pretending. i am offering opportunities to feel

taken, like *one's breath away* or

by the experience of : as in : take my paayals,
reader, my silver cups, my tarnished

bangles. try to fit

them, narrow, around
your wrists. tell me

you feel free.

coldplay goes to india to shoot during holi & i just have to keep living my life

carrying on collecting prayers, repeating *om shanti* & imagining i'm
inside some pastel temple. white peacocks flash their beaks
in the verdant anywhere, & the boy cranking a megaphone
his mother painted blue & poppy with a dried grass
paintbrush—he has a name, receives no check-per-play
& on youtube a male commenter writes, *travel to india
is one of my dreams, this video makes it stronger.* i vow & vow
against this *hymn*—slow motion & splicing & for some reason
beyoncé lording over slums. *drunk & high* when she gestures
a clumsy bharatanatyam—all draped dupatta, metallic lip gloss—
i'm being too extra in public again. yes, i want permission
to take it back—her airbrushed crown, our wedding jewelry
—but here are so many white faces, tilted up as in ecstasy, & i can't
argue, there is a certain pleasure in consuming packaged
otherness, like catching the bouquet when there's already a ring
on your finger. no point asking for what won't be given. instead
i pray : no bharat as a scene up for the taking. as they say
in the states, bless your *head full of dreams* for visiting.
my eyes are closed & i won't lose my temper, want a world
where my people aren't background, refuse to be an extra
in someone else's *weekend* again. like the scene, timeworn,

where my white ex queues up bollywood compilations,
screws an invisible bulb, laughs & later
punches me in the face. how i forgot & was then
reminded : this was his shot. again i am lost & cannot help
but leave the bar, walk myself down the street,
my mother's prayers the soundtrack to my slow journey
home. & still am haunted by caricature. an old-school film reel.
low-cut red gown barely holding in bey's tits. a bunch of villagers
eating this shit up. christopher, i'm begging you, take off
your mandala-clad leather jacket. all this playing dress up *got me
feeling* i'm trapped in the story of every white boy's colorful past,
sitting in a plush theater seat, watching my own life
derail. wipe the color off your face, chris. let your legs wind you
backward, onto the plane. let the garlands not be props.
let kids on concrete roofs smile & re-palm that ethereal paint,
crowd around someone who's less of a ghost.
romance something of your own.

pastoral with keys clenched, as a weapon, in my fist

how the fat pink blossoms smell of sex & the season
when girls all cower has passed. onward

in the dimming light, i hold the dog close to my side
with a tether. i am followed by such a train of *ooh's* &
before me the white boys on the fourth floor unfurl

their only emblem, their same-colors-as-acceptable-
pride : reconfiguration of stripes to flatten. what women

should wear & how : what a country should wear
& when. if i wrap myself in flags or if i wrap myself
in many warnings. if i point to the dog at my side

when making eye contact with any of the same
type who held me against a brick wall. how the fat

squirrels don't duck when the dog lunges
toward them, & i think without thinking, *another species
asking to die.* fat pink blossom, sex emblem,

pepper-spraying my way through america : i am
my survival instinct or i am not

my survival instinct. daily i learn : reconfigure the self
as almost-not-killable, almost-not-
fuckable. keep walking & take stock of my

surroundings. only dead girls check their phones.
i am a fat pink sex symbol. i agree with you.

summoning : ways you asked for it

you begin to feel an affinity for plants, especially
in winter, their pot-laden roots thick with rime

their spiked plumage mesmerizes : not
an invitation. you : all familiar with that disposition

+

were you in a village
or deep in a borough
either way was the street
dark never mind you know
the streets darken when women walk alone
& knowing this you do what you've been told
you *should be absolutely fine* doing

you put your cigarette out in philadelphia's eye

+

no one told you about your molten
flesh, how it slinks off itself
like snakeskin. you start to avoid pink

because through until there's no oxygen left,
you're made of it. color the setting sun
slush gray. you know how to make nothing

out of something, know how to walk
your swoon-blank block

+

dust floats in the air above you, the mattress

you count shells like a rosary

you suspect several oceans brought you here
then abandoned you salt-rimmed & pining

you thumb the oyster's obsidian

jodhpur, jharkhand, philadelphia

the air is writ of ash & sand, though this
is no memorial. camels buckle clumsily

      groundward   & i've forgotten

how to grieve. i was nowhere
when my grandparents

      died, just like i'm nowhere

now, picturing jain temples & carved
elephants & the faces

      of so many monkeys huddled

on eaves. i wish all women on earth
a day of invisible. i wish for no

      trials, no catcalls, no

sound. like how i am
on this dune : transparent   wondering

      about power & numbers. bodies

of accused women go unreported
while i roast dough over dull

      heat. this in the country   empire left

behind. here,
the flour-silted air. here, the warm, dry scent

      of pyre. i'm moving, now, through paved

streets, all old film & detergent, kept aloft
by gusts from subway grates, wondering

      how the river smells when women

are dragged   into it, the pink city turning
blue at dusk, sandstone   falling   into music.

      at a wedding in the west, my great aunt celebrates

her sister's death : spirits, she sings,
are all around us. good & evil & will

      we lend an open ear. here is my plea

on cue : country of drought
& several gods, country of waterfalls

      wrung brown with soil's unease, i'm not there

enough, not you   enough
& i've come to ask   what to do

      with our dead. rivermouth

& useless, reading up   on reportage, i'm by

a stream or in
the desert   or dragging my scent

through the unwashed city : what good

is brotherly love   what good
is empire   paving over

             ground   bones, i don't know why

my story matters, i don't know
why   this story.

summoning : ash in my palms, ash on the streets

reeking of moss & blossom & on the street
i call home, i cannot be sure i
exist. thighs press one another

& it is in essence a grounding—here, my shorts
and sheer top—& i pass a minivan, no color
in particular, its doors & trunk

open, interior filled with funerary
bouquets, satin ribbons spilling
out the back, white & red & yellow bulbs & so

many stems. i'm thinking about support,
what makes me possible here, next
to the colonnades, the mourning

filing unceremoniously out to smoke
on the front steps in dresses i think to myself
are too short for lament—   then challenge

my inner oppressor
again. thirteen months since we scattered
Dadaji's ashes. i'm reminded : no ceremony

does justice. i walk on & keep
grieving everything i see,
there & here.

+

preparing for some Q&A i face

        myself frontal, hair in curlers
        & vegetable oil, the way

i was taught, Ma's fingers kneading

        my supple dough, thin skin,
        silly skull. only so many poems come

each year. women, i feel

        a pressing, & yet some days— . here's
        what happens when i shirk your pain.

i wrestle each clip from its clamp

        & hold. the curls
        fall away & i'm on camera,

limp. i'm sitting next to myself.

        she speaks for me. i hate her mouth,
        what issues forth, how she's miming

some woman i've yet to adore.

+

i use the wrong spelling of the american
word because, yeah, i guess technically

i've been owned by the english? my love retorts
meaning nothing of it : "didn't you grow up here?" yes,

me & my language learning app, me & my kajal
at noon under the comcast building. yes, disguised

as tamarind, i'm all loll. i'm nothing
if not your tongue

& how i adhere to it without asking
any questions, any questions at all.

+

mortuaries & i sit nestled behind
thick curtains, air conditioner blaring

  my privilege like a siren.

ran from a man across the street again
tonight, followed other immigrants' names

  home—gangemi, baldi, grasso.

he tracked my weaving through a maze
of parked cars, called me "snack," then

  "cunt." i live in the empire

   & peace is illusion

    everywhere.

+

alone online, i hunt for more
motherland. am starved
for belonging. will never

belong. Ma would say : "wherever you are,
you're home." i find a video of men
in kerala palming short glass

cups of tea. their fingers claw
the edges, flip upside-down & back
& milk sifts like a drunk cloud

into chai, cardamom pods swirling
to surface despite the inverted
tornado. skinny brown things

with star-shaped crowns, bobbing
in the white. i'm tired, don't transcribe
the metaphor.

+

of the role of silence in this world

                    i want to write something like : who violences

            us, who palms our tender

skulls & plucks us

from the silver tray.

here i am trying

to hold on to my head.

+

i summon the version of your
masc, love, that does not

exoticize or point out, yeah,

my on-stage persona
is really indian, almost as if

i myself am indian. "that's why

i want my nose pierced," i'd said
at sixteen—stoned on the good high

of not eating & disappearing white—

Ma in the hospital
riddled with malaria, "i want to feel

connected."

i make a toothpick diadem & crown myself token

pink light sears the marbled bar & the straw in my drink
is pastel. on wood-paneled walls, american traditional paintings
of my goddesses. kati texts me, *all this gaslighting*
today. i'm taking extra space, my bags all over
the butterscotch seats, & the only men around are behind
the bar, burning sage & lemon rinds for garnish, talking
about mangoes—their remedial qualities, the cost & palette &
current trend toward. i'm turning fuchsia, bottled up.
appropriate me sideways, my bags are full & i'm nothing
if not a product, lush. kati writes, *like how i'm feeling*
isn't legitimate enough. on the counter, two artificial flames
are a native woman's breasts. durga save me, i'm liable
to paint the borough white—that is, in reminder—my wrists
already smelling of tamarind & jasmine & not because
it comes natural, but if i'm to invest in anything, shouldn't
it be our first fruit, that ancient juice, & shouldn't it be
to remedy—. i have to cherry-pick my battles here, can't argue
against exotic existence, so i don't write, *my mother*
holding a mango is more brown joy than this place will ever see.
filaments fitted with paisleys glow & the tequila's got this sweet
bite & i'm pissed at the walls, they just shutter out
light. joy is fine, joy is pretty pink, but kati *would like to yell,*
after all, isn't dissent patriotic & anger a form of grief

& i inhale the incense the white bartender burns as if
from a censer. my holy hour has only just begun. yes,
mangoes are astonishing & women are worth
our own saving. i go about separating pulp
from rind.

summoning : second chakra

i bless it for sharing my ochre, for its scent—turmeric
& faintly golden. for distorted grapefruit & its rumbling
in the spools of me when i've hit deep red
too many nights & accumulating. i bless hunger
because it, too, is bittersweet, like cicadas humming me
to sleep bedside. who knows how long they'll survive.
i summon shade, for i've been satiated with sun
& damn human that i am, i keep leaving my tattoos
uncovered, keep up my solar addiction. hell, bless them both,
bless all my eventual liver spots & the amber paint
i'll someday dapple onto my self-portraits accordingly.
bless all the animals i love that have eyes which change color
slightly depending on the quality of cloud. for this
like every era is one i'm not sure i will survive & orange
almost means the very boiling of it. even so, bless this sweet
apricot seed, currant bite at my core, what have i done wrong
but lust & want, & how can i not swallow all the chakra offers
with daybreak & then the steady thawing. o ray, o dappling,
o watered-down, the clouds in future storms will be fuchsia
perhaps & certainly i'll have to document, if i survive i'll want
to look back & relive every burn, & this, this, this one too.

at home, in the empire

the patio at this bar births brown ladybugs
& i'm burning my mouth for fun. on the edges

      of desi women's lips—milk souring, some liquor

to help us forget. cities in america & i
am tired. villages back home : i squint & almost

      belong & train cars rattle, peopled,

my god, limbs everywhere. call this day *scant* & hear
the letters wrong. call me *foreign*

      & god have i complied. women i'd call *sister,*

i see you. there's soot coating rails & the heat
is our house & i can't rid this book

      of my life, & we're all coins left in fountains

making language of strife. alina's name is a song
& she knows it, & i'm veering political

      over cardamom at the bar, i gesture with my hands

& it is universal, i ask, what are we stained by
if not our love of men?

      where do we go at sunset? who sees us

on the ground in the dark, clouds of dust
in our wake, shuffling to or from ourselves? my mouth

is on fire & i light the thing backwards

& alina says today is the day of three-hundred hugs
just between us. she's got a bottle

in her hand & the posture

of an immigrant & i won't rid this book
of our lives. this poem is about

recognition. this poem : wishful

thinking. women, i want it to be
believable : that we leave the bar, the sky stupid

with gold. that no one follows us home.

Notes

"on projection"
Beginning with this poem & for the rest of the book, I am writing, in part, in conversation with Paisley Rekdal's *Appropriate: A Provocation* (W. W. Norton, 2020). In many ways, Rekdal's text could be considered further reading for *summonings*.

"lucky inhabitant"
[In response to...what instigated a particular {witch} hunt], [almost all of the participants...interviewed] by one anthropologist said, [*"Ki jani?!"*], as in, who knows why these attacks occur? Or, as one respondent said, ["Who knows?! Who knows what the old hag (*buria*) did! I do not know."]

Influenced in part by Christine Blasey Ford's testimony, this poem would also not exist without Victoria Chang's book, *Barbie Chang*.

"ghazal against [declining to name the subject]"
[In almost all cases, the identity of the witch is that of a local village woman whose reputation can be easily maligned through accusations of witchcraft. In a matter of a few hours, through gossip, rumor, and conspiracy, the entire village then blames her for the misfortunes] the village is currently experiencing. As Jharkhand Assembly party whip, Radha Krishna Kishore, stated in 2016, "People here brand a woman witch and kill her even when the village well goes dry in summer."

Bracketed material in this poem's title comes from Susan Sontag's seminal text on the politics of viewing images of suffering & atrocity, *Regarding the Pain of Others*.

"ojha : rituals"
[For the worker community of tea plantations {*adivasis*}, the moral order is defined through beliefs in spirits, and all harm...is directed towards the handiwork of the witch or other supernatural causes.] The community believes that [the invisible world is filled with spirits that cause diseases and illness; these are the darker spirits. The central idea is to seek an alliance with the helpful white spirits.]

"we don't belong"
In communities where witch hunting is practiced, [women are considered impure and menstruation is seen as an outlet for their sins. Particular care is taken that no menstruating woman even casts her shadow on the images of gods.]

"to curse or to pray"
Goddess Kali is primarily associated with both sexuality & violence. [This kind of polarity is used to define goddesses and women in Hinduism...on the one hand, the woman is fertile, benevolent—the bestower; on the other, she is aggressive, malevolent—the destroyer.] The poem posits a connection between Kali and women accused of being witches; see note for "daayan & the mountains : i" for further explanation.

Lyrics from folk songs also appear in this piece; [it is believed that the witches dance and sing together on certain days, and that they have their own songs for these occasions.]

"at first, trying to reach those accused"
[Faced with poor wages and the associated dismal living and working conditions that accompany a suppressed working class...the *adivasi*

workers connect the micro-, village-level strain of ailments to witchcraft rather than blaming the deaths on the lack of proper medical aid for the workers.] Forces noted as having influenced this culture of accusation include: land disputes, [anti-colonial tensions], [fear and suspicion of women's sexuality], &, more broadly, [gender conflicts legitimized by religion, folklore, and patriarchal customs].

"daayan senses the ojha"
[The accused women are mostly childless widows who have a life interest in their lands (i.e., a right to control the land and its production that will, after their death, pass on to their nearest male relative).]

"daayan after a village feast"
[Women's knowledge of herbs and plants, particularly medicinal ones, is considered a precious family possession.] In a discussion with an anthropologist, [one woman said, 'Sometimes we take a bottle of liquor in our basket, and drink together in the forest.' The forest as a social place where women went in groups to collect firewood, gossip, eat, sing, roam, bathe, and escape from household chores, has shrunk over time.]

"the tea leaves"
[Women work in the fields as 'tea-leaf pickers'.] Echoing the dichotomous nature of Goddess Kali, Dakini, & women accused of being witches (see note for "daayan & the mountains : i" below), [women's work on the plantations is simultaneously fetishized, romanticized (nimble fingers suitable for plucking), and devalued.]

"daayan, feet facing forward" & "the villagers' story"
[As understood and depicted by men, eating symbolizes the 'destructive' power of women.] An anonymous male villager elaborated in 2015, "The

witches eat human flesh and drink human blood. That's what our elders have seen." Another male villager, Maniyar Buria, said this in 2009 regarding the identification of witches, "You can see it in their eyes. They have different eyes."

"daayan & the mountains : i"
Dakini's meaning seems to have evolved over time in these [patrilineal agriculturist communities]. Commonly known to be one of Kali's associates, Dakini refers to [a curved female goblin who represents female supremacy on earth]. Simultaneously, [Dakini Vidya means witchcraft. So Dakini's knowledge is the knowledge of the witch]. Dakini's association both with Goddess Kali & with witchcraft begs the question, [Why and how did the meaning of the word witch, dan or dakin, reverse diametrically? What are the social factors responsible for its transformation from a word of respect and awe to a word of abuse and hatred?]

"the village goddess talks to herself while applying kohl," "daayan imagines herself as the village goddess", & "daayan summons the village goddess"
Inside patriarchal cultures where witch hunting is practiced, women can [derive power and status by claiming to be possessed by the spirit of the goddess, 'to effectively resist oppression.'] In one representative case, [a self-proclaimed goddess accused Purni Orang of performing black magic and causing disease and death...Purni Orang, 63, was dragged from her house by a mob, beaten up, stripped, and beheaded for being a witch.]

"daayan at gold streak river"
Researchers describe a marriage song that idolizes the village ojha as follows: [The witch-finder suffocates the witch to death by forcibly

submerging her in the river...The witch stands for the women's right to knowledge and access to cultivation and the witch-finder represents the male dominance over land, knowledge, and agriculture in the community...The purpose is to caution the young bride against nurturing any thoughts about claiming her husband's property (land and water sources). The song...is, in fact, a superb example of the ritual humiliation of women, expressing the male ideology of the indigenous society.]

"the village men find some [fellowship], [hunt]"

Two key dynamics to consider when reading this poem are detailed here. First, [the *adivasi* migrant group is also caught in the bigger conspiracy of the plantation owners and management, who manipulate the witchcraft associations and witch hunts that follow as means to further isolate the community from the mainstream population with constructed images of primitiveness and wildness that get legitimized by the witchcraft accusations that take place.] Second, [lynching's particular vocabulary—the social air to its undertaking, the near-ceremonial bloodshed, the display of the mutilated body in triumph—belongs to the category of crime committed by men against those they see as property. As a punishment, it is a work of collective fiction: a gang of imagined victims wreaking vengeance on an imagined criminal in an inversion of the truth.]

"[every woman is a potential witch]"

This poem would not exist without Elissa Washuta's essay, "White Witchery," which first appeared in *Guernica,* nor without Vanessa Angélica Villarreal's essay, "Witchcraft is Capitalism's New Trick," which first appeared in *bitch media.* As Villarreal notes, [U.S. witches are still the witches of empire.]

"god of new beginnings, i celebrate you poorly"
This poem refers to & was composed on Ganesh Chaturthi. In it, the speaker grapples with the fact that, in India as in America, [women cope within patriarchal constraints with strategies that involve making bargains towards the goal of maximizing financial security and life options.] An anthropologist further specifies: [*adivasi* women…bargain their domestic service, which includes listening and supporting her husband without question, in return for economic and social support from him.]

"coldplay goes to india to shoot during holi & i just have to keep living my life"
Lyrics from Coldplay's "Hymn for the Weekend" & comments on its YouTube music video are italicized. This poem would not exist without Shayla Lawson's poem, "Nights," nor without Traci Brimhall's poem, "The Unconfirmed Miracles at Puraquequara."

"jodhpur, jharkhand, philadelphia"
This poem would not exist without Cathy Linh Che's poem, "Los Angeles, Manila, Đà Nẵng."

"summoning : ash in my palms, ash on the streets"
This poem is dedicated to my maternal grandparents.

+

Direct quotations from accused women, male villagers, & Jharkhand Assembly members were sampled from the following sources:

Masoodi, Ashwaq. "Witch Hunting | Victims of superstition." *LiveMint,* February 23, 2014.

Singh, Shiv Sahay. "The 'witches' of Jharkhand." *The Hindu,* December 24, 2016.

Tamin, Baba. "Magazine: Meet the Indian women hunted as witches." *Al Jazeera*, June 5, 2015.

Anthropological research throughout is cast in the poet's original language, except for bracketed text, which was sampled from the following sources:

Chaudhuri, Soma. *Witches, Tea Plantations, and Lives of Migrant Laborers in India: Tempest in a Teapot.* Lexington Books, 2013.

Goldsmith, Belinda, and Meka Beresford. "Exclusive: India most dangerous country for women with sexual violence rife – global poll." *Thomson Reuters.* June 25, 2018.

Matthan, Ayesha. "Woman or Goddess?" *Indian Divine: Gods and Goddesses in 19th and 20th century Indian Art,* 2014.

Mullick, Samar Bosu. "Gender Relations and Witches among the Indigenous Communities of Jharkhand, India." *Gender Relations in Forest Societies in Asia: Patriarchy at Odds.* Kelkar, Govind, and Dev Nathan and Pierre Walter, editors. SAGE Publications, 2004.

Munshi, Indra. "Women and Forest: A Study of the Warlis of Western India." *Gender Relations in Forest Societies in Asia: Patriarchy at Odds.* Kelkar, Govind, and Dev Nathan and Pierre Walter, editors. SAGE Publications, 2004.

Nair, Supriya. "The Meaning of India's 'Beef Lynchings.'" *The Atlantic.* July 24, 2017.

Santoshini, Sarita. "Hunting down witches in northeast India." *Al Jazeera.* September 3, 2015.

Shaffer, Ryan. "Modern Witch Hunting and Superstitious Murder in India." *The Skeptical Inquirer.* July/August 2014.

Siegel, James. *Naming the Witch.* Stanford University Press, 2006.

Taseer, Aatish. "Can the World's Largest Democracy Endure Another Five Years of a Modi Government?" *Time Magazine.* May 9, 2019.

Glossary of Terms

+ *Adivasi*: migrant communities of plantation workers. [Witchcraft accusations are a way for the adivasi workers to get control over their lives within the exploitative nature of plantations]

+ *Bhaiya*: brother

+ *Bonga:* evil spirit; [in copulation, the vagina is sometimes described as 'like a bonga']

+ *Daayan(s) / dain /dan / dakan(i):* interchangeable terms across dialects for a witch; in this text, *daayan* refers to a woman who has been accused of being a witch

+ *Haria*: [rice beer, the most sacred as well as favorite drink of the people]

+ *Jaher era:* the matron of the sacred grove

+ *Nage era:* the matron of water

+ *Ojha / bhagat / janguru:* interchangeable terms across dialects for a medicine man

+ *Paje:* [a watery gruel made from rice] that adivasi subsist on [during the lean season...March to May]

+ *Planter's raj:* [control of labor supply, rail, and coal fell under special laws that gave the British planters unlimited power] until 1947 (Indian Independence)

Acknowledgments

Gratitude to the editors of the following journals, where these poems first appeared, often in younger versions and sometimes by a different name:

Academy of American Poets' Poem-A-Day: "ojha : rituals"

American Poetry Review: "at first, trying to reach the accused," "before plantations, women rustle the brush together," & "daayan senses the ojha"

ANOMALY: "daayan after a village feast" & "we don't belong"

Asian American Writers' Workshop: "coldplay goes to india to shoot during holi & i just have to keep living my life"

bedfellows: "pastoral with keys clenched, as a weapon, in my fist"

Blackbird: "daayan, feet facing forward"

BOAAT: "daayan summons the village 'goddess'"

Crazyhorse: "ghazal against [declining to name the subject]" & "[every woman is a potential witch]"

Day One: "summoning : ways you asked for it" ("scenario three : ways you asked for it")

Diode: "daayan at gold streak river" & "on persona"

Foundry: "daayan conjures up a forest"

Grist: "the villagers' story" & "the village goddess talks to herself while applying kohl"

Massachusetts Review: "the mountains speak to the village"

The Nation: "i make a toothpick diadem & crown myself token"

The Rumpus: "jodhpur, jharkhand, philadelphia" & "god of new beginnings, i celebrate you poorly"

SC BIPOC Anthology, Muddy Ford Press: "summoning : retreat"

The Shallow Ends: "daayan & the mountains : i"

Stirrings: "summoning : you are not a myth" ("scenario five : you are not a myth")

Tinderbox: "at home in the empire," "summoning : you didn't submerge your head in the river" ("scenario one : you didn't submerge your head in the river,") & "summoning : wanderless" ("scenario two : wanderless")

Tupelo Quarterly Review: "on projection," "the mountains recall the myth," & "daayan looks to the earth"

Virginia Quarterly Review: "garba, or womb + lamp, or as in every tradition there is a woman & her body & both are vessels," "the universe will end & kali will still be here," "the village men find some [fellowship], [hunt]," "summoning with chai & failure," & "summoning : ash in my palms, ash on the streets"

+

Additional gratitude to the editors of the following anthologies, where these poems were reprinted:

Poetry Daily: "daayan at gold streak river"

The Familiar Wild: On Dogs & Poetry: "pastoral with keys clenched, as a weapon, in my fist"

The Penguin Book of Modern Indian Poets: "garba, or womb + lamp, or as in every tradition there is a woman & her body & both are vessels," "at first, trying to reach those accused," "daayan at gold streak river," "at home, in the empire," "i make a toothpick diadem & crown myself token," & "lucky inhabitant"

They Rise Like A Wave: An Anthology of Asian American Women Poets (Blue Oak Press): "lucky inhabitant"

+

Thank you to my editor Diane Goettel, for believing in this project & in my vision for the book. Special thanks to Meera Dugal for the cover art for *summonings*.

I cannot express enough gratitude for the generous guidance of these wonderful humans, without whom there would simply be no book of which to speak: Elissa Washuta, Hanif Abdurraqib, Ariana Reines, Alina Pleskova, Gala Mukomolova, Nomi Stone, Ali Pearl, Shelley Wong, Cait Weiss, Cindy Arrieu-King, Chantz Erolin, Emma Brown Sanders, Megan Peak, Kathy Fagan, Emily Rosko, Trevor Ketner, Carly Joy Miller, Danielle DeTiberus, KMA Sullivan. Thank you to the Philadelphia writers & artists, too many to name here, who first welcomed me & continue to inspire me; you have utterly changed the way I define community.

To the poets at The Home School—Myung Mi Kim, Douglas Kearney, Dorothea Lasky, Geoffery G. O'Brien, & Harryette Mullen—& to the friends I made in Hudson, thank you for helping ignite the spark that became this project. Thanks, too, to Sundress Academy for the Arts— the farmhouse goats make a special appearance in two of these poems! For the time, space, breath, & greenery this book needed to begin to grow, thank you to Bucknell University—namely, K.A. Hays, Andrew Ciotola, G.C. Waldrep, Mary Ruefle, & David Winter. Special thanks *VIDA* & *PEN America*, & the myriad wonderful students & faculty I've encountered & been altered by while performing with these poems.

To my friends, family, & colleagues, thank you, thank you, thank you for your unconditional love & support. Gratitude to Mike and Harley, my heart. Y'all keep making every day possible.

Finally, I acknowledge the women, men, and children across the globe whose lives are affected by witch hunting. I end where I began, with fragments & attempts. My final offering is a title from Audre Lorde: "There Are No Honest Poems About Dead Women."

Photo: Brooke Marsh

Raena Shirali is the author of two collections of poetry. Her first book, *GILT* (YesYes Books, 2017), won the 2018 Milt Kessler Poetry Book Award, and her second, *summonings* (Black Lawrence Press, 2022), won the 2021 Hudson Prize. Winner of a Pushcart Prize & a former Philip Roth Resident at Bucknell University, Shirali is also the recipient of prizes and honors from VIDA, *Gulf Coast, Boston Review,* & *Cosmonauts Avenue*. Formerly a Co-Editor-in-Chief of *Muzzle Magazine*, Shirali now serves as Faculty Advisor for *Folio*—a literary magazine dedicated to publishing works by undergraduate students at the national level. She holds an MFA in Poetry from The Ohio State University and is an Assistant Professor of English at Holy Family University. The Indian American poet was raised in Charleston, South Carolina, and now lives in Philadelphia.